YIDDISH

WITH

GEORGE AND LAURA

YIDDISH

WITH

GEORGE AND LAURA

Ellis Weiner
Barbara Davilman

Illustrations by Larry Ruppert

Little, Brown and Company
New York Boston London

Little, Brown and Company
Hachette Book Group USA
1271 Avenue of the Americas, New York, NY 10020
Visit our Web site at HachetteBookGroupUSA.com

First Edition: October 2006

Library of Congress Cataloging-in-Publication Data

Weiner, Ellis.
  Yiddish with George and Laura / Ellis Weiner and Barbara Davilman. –
1st ed.
     p. cm.
  ISBN-10: 0-316-01446-X
  ISBN-13: 978-0-316-01446-5
  1. Bush, George W. (George Walker), 1946– Humor. 2. Bush, Laura
Welch, 1946– Humor. 3. Bush family—Humor. 4. WASPs (Persons) — Humor.
5. Yiddish language — Humor. I. Davilman, Barbara. II. Title.
  E903.3.W45 2006
  973.931092'2–dc22   2006018513

10 9 8 7 6 5 4 3 2 1

WOR
Book Design by Meryl Sussman Levavi
Printed in the United States of America

YIDDISH

WITH

GEORGE AND LAURA

See George.

He is our president.

He lives in a fancy white house
and is a big *shmegegge*.

George loves his job.

He gets to take a lot of vacations.

He gets to do special things for his
family and friends.

"Not bad for an ex-*shikker*,"
he thinks.

See Laura.

She is George's wife.

She loves George very much.

She is a nice lady and a *shiksa*.

See Jenna and Barbara.

They are George and Laura's twin daughters.

They are a couple of *sheyna maidls*.

Jenna was cited two times for underage drinking.

Barbara was cited only once.

George and Laura *shepn naches* from their lovely girls.

Shept, George and Laura, *shept*.
Shept, shept, shept.

George and Laura and the girls
are going to a birthday party for
George's parents.
Their birthdays are four days apart.
The party is at the family house
in Kennebunkport.

Kennebunkport is a pretty town
in Maine.
A lot of *goyim* live there.

See George's mother.

Her name is Bar.

She wears a lot of pearls and
is a *farbissenah*.

"You are late, George," Bar says.

"Of course I am late," George says.
"I am the president of the United
States.
I am a big *macher*."

"I do not care," says Bar.
"You should have been here
two hours ago.
Doro and the wives got tired
of waiting.
They went shopping for
tchotchkies."

"We want to go shopping too,"
says Jenna.

"But you just got here," says Bar.

"We want to spend money and help
the economy," says Barbara.

"Oh, all right," says Bar.
"But stay away from the *farkaktah*
media."

"Where is Dad?" asks George.
He holds out a flag.
"I got this for him."

"He does not want
that flag, George,"
says Bar.
"If he did he would have gotten one
himself.
But I will put it in the den with all
our other *chazerai*."

See Jeb.

Jeb is one of George's brothers.
Jeb is the governor of Florida.
He helped George win the
elections.
He is an avid golfer and a *finagler*.

"Mom is mad at you, George," says Jeb.

"Hey, Jeb," says George.

 "How is your daughter, Noelle? Is she still taking Ex-Lax and smoking that *farshlugginer* crack?"

"You do not mean Ex-Lax,"
says Jeb.
"You mean Xanax.
No, she is off drugs and in therapy."

"*Therapy schmerapy*,"
says George.
"If someone has troubles they should talk to God."

See Neil.

He is George's brother, too.

He was in the savings and loan business.

A lot of people lost money at his bank.

They were very sad.

Neil made a lot of money at his bank and was very happy.

Now Neil does this and that and is *epes* a *nudnik*.

"How are you, Neil?" says George.

"I am fine," says Neil.
"I am working hard on my
educational software company."

"That is wonderful,"
says George.
"I am interested in
education, too.
I am making sure
that no child
gets left
behind."

"But what if a child DOES get left behind?" asks Neil.

"Then he can join the army," says George. *"Nifter-schmifter, a leben macht er?"*

See Marvin.

He is another one of George's brothers.

He was a board member of a large security company.

They were helping to keep the World Trade Center safe.

Now he owns stock in a company that makes money thanks to the Patriot Act.

Marvin is a real *goen*.

"Mom wants everyone to come in for lunch," says Marvin.

"I am not hungry, George," says Laura.
"You eat lunch.
I will just *shpotzir* for a while."

See Laura *shpotzir*.
Shpotzir, Laura, *shpotzir*.
Shpotzir, *shpotzir*, *shpotzir*.

George, Jeb, Neil, and Marvin sit
in the dining room.
Bar brings out chicken croquettes,
stuffed baked potatoes, and
succotash.
All the food is the same color.

"This food looks delicious, Mother," says Neil.

"Oh shut up, Neil," George says. "You little *tuchas leker*."

Bar tastes the food.
"This food is NOT delicious,"
says Bar.
"It is absolutely *chalushisdick*."

"It is not that bad, Mother," says Marvin.

"Yes it is!" says Bar.
"George was so late that the croquettes are completely *farfalen*."

"You are right, Mother," says Jeb.
"And the potatoes are *gornisht helfn*."

"I was late because I am a very important person," says George.
"My job is hard work and I am doing it very well.
I am making sure everyone is getting *ongeshtopt mit gelt*."

"That is what you should do,
George," says Bar.
"You are helping your family and
friends.
It is the least you can do after you
have been an *umglick* all your life."

"Oh yeah?" says George.
"I am doing more than Dad ever did."

Bar says, "Here comes your father. So *shvayg*."

See Poppy!

Poppy is the father of George, Jeb, Marvin, Neil, and their sister, Doro. He is Bar's husband.

"Smells good, Bar," says Poppy.

"Dad, Mom is not being nice," says George.

"Listen to your mother," says
Poppy.
"She is in charge of the *kinder*."

"I am more than just one of the children," says George.

"I was elected twice. I was given a mandate."

"You do not even know what a mandate is, George," says Jeb. "You think it is when two *faygelahs* go to the movies."

"Do not tease George," says Marvin.

"Or he will go back to blowing up frogs."

"Do not listen to
them, George,"
says Neil.
"They do not know
what it is like to run
a country."

"And now we never will," says Jeb.
"You have ruined it for the rest
of us."

"Oh yeah, Jeb and
Marvin?"
George says.
"You can *kush mir
in tuchas*."

Laura walks through the woods.
In mitt'n drinen she sees
something on the ground.

It is a baby.

"I will take you home to George,"
Laura says.
"He loves children.
He thinks they are a *brocheh*."

George goes into the den.

He is angry.

George gets thirsty when he is angry.

Bar calls from the dining room.

"George!" she says.

"Come have dessert!"

George is startled.

He spills the drink.

"Uh-oh," he says.

"I need this like a *loch in kop*."

George sees the flag he brought
for his father.

He uses the flag to wipe up the
spill.

He looks at the floor and thinks he
has done a fine job.

"*Alts iz gut*," he says.

George stuffs the wet flag under the sofa.

"George!" his mother calls. "Where are you?"

"I am going upstairs," George says. "I am going to take a *shluf.*"

George lies down in his room.
Laura comes in.
She has the baby with her.

"Look what I found, George!"
she says.
"Can we keep him?"

"Laura," says George.
"*Bist meshugeh?*"

"I would love to take this baby in,"
George says.
"You know how much I am for
children.
But we have to be strong.

If we take this baby in, it sends a
bad message.
Pretty soon everyone will be
having babies and leaving them
in the woods for someone else
to take care of.
Umbashrien!"

Laura takes the baby back to the woods.

She puts it on the ground.

"I am sorry it did not work out," she says.

"But *s' iz geven a fargenign aykh tsu zen.*"

George is just about to fall asleep.
He hears a knock on the door.

It is Jeb.
"Mom wants to see you in the den,"
Jeb says.
"You are in trouble up to your
kishkes."

"Look what you did, George,"
Bar says.
She points to the floor.
"This is a *kaporah!*"

"What is?" asks George.
"The rug has always been like this."

"George, you have a lot of *chutzpah*," says Marvin.

"The rug was not like this," Bar
says.
"Something was spilled on it today.
It is still wet.
And you did it."

"I did not do it," George says.
"But if I did do it,
I had a very good reason."

"Oh no, George," Bar says.
"Do not give me your usual *shtik*."

"You must fix this," says Bar.
"It is time for you to grow up.
It is time for you to stop being such
a *shmendrik*."

Laura walks back from the woods.
She sees Poppy and starts to cry.

"What is wrong, Laura?" Poppy
asks.
"You seem a tad *farklemt.*"

Laura tells Poppy about the baby.

"Do not feel bad, Laura,"
Poppy says.
"Saving babies is
not our job."

"What is our
job, Poppy?"
Laura asks.

"Tell people
what they
want to hear.
Then take all
you can get,"
says Poppy.
"Now *genug* with that crying."

Laura thinks Poppy is the wisest *shver* in the world.

"It is all fixed," says George.

"That was quick," says Jeb.
"How did you fix it?"

"Hey, Jeb," says George.
"Why don't you bite my *shvants?*"

Everyone hears a loud thud!
Then there is a *geshrai*.

"*Oy!*"

See Poppy.

"Are you all right?" Bar asks.

"I don't know how this globe got here," Poppy says.
"I feel like a *shlimazel.*"

"Why, what is this?" Jeb asks.
"There is a big stain in the middle
of the rug.
I wonder where it came from."

"I wonder, too," says Marvin.
"Whoever did this is really *af tsores*."

George looks at Bar.

Bar looks at
George.

"Oh, that Juanita," Bar says.
"She must have moved the globe
when she was cleaning.
She is very *shlumperdik*."

"Juanita?" Jeb says.

Bar looks at Jeb.
"Yes," she says. "Juanita.
She is the maid."

"But where did the stain come
from?" Marvin asks.

"Juanita spilled a drink," Bar says.
"Then she covered it up with the
globe."

"That is a shame," says George.
"But *azoy vert dos kichl
tzekrochen!*"

"You will have to let her go, Bar," says Poppy.

"That is not fair," Marvin says.

"Marvin is right," says Jeb.
"How do we know Juanita did it?"

"We know," says Bar.

"*Farshtayst?*"
George says.
He sticks his
tongue out at
Jeb and
Marvin.

"Listen, Jeb and Marvin and Neil,"
Bar says.
"Doro and the wives and all our
friends will be here soon.
Clean up this *hekdish*."

Laura sees Jenna and Bar
through the window.
"The girls are back," she
"Let's go help them with their
bags."

"Loo...

k at what we found!"
enna says.

Laura looks at the blanket.
"Where did you get this?" she asks.

"It was wrapped around a baby
in the woods," says Jenna.

"What did you do
with the baby?"
Laura asks.

"Oh, we left
the baby
there,"
says
Barbara.

"If we had brought the baby home, then everybody would have babies and leave them in the woods for other people to take care of."

"*Zeyer sheyn gezogt!*" George says.

"Besides," Jenna says.
"All we wanted was the blanket."

"Aren't our girls great, Laura?"
asks George.
"We did a heck of a job!"

"You always do, George," says
Laura.
"You always do."

But that is a whole other *megillah*.

Authors' Note

Yiddish with George and Laura is, like *Ragtime* by E. L. Doctorow, the *Commedia* by Dante Alighieri, and *The Tragedy of Julius Caesar* by William Shakespeare, a fictional story populated by real, nonfictional individuals. True, reasonable people may disagree about how "real" some of its protagonists are, but it is at least beyond dispute that they are nonfictional.

As we did in *Yiddish with Dick and Jane*, we have placed Yiddish words and phrases in the mouths of characters not normally associated with that language, with Jewish culture, or with the kinds of rueful emotional truths and ironic social commentary for which Yiddish is one of the world's most supple and nuanced means of expression. No, no one bet us we could not produce a book about George and Laura containing the phrase "supple and nuanced means of expression," but if they had, we would have just won.

There will be those who wonder what the point of all this is. Let's just say that we officiated over this shotgun marriage of one of America's most prominent, or at least powerful, families and an aging tribal language from Eastern Europe for two reasons:

One, we thought it would be funny, and in a particularly satisfying way.

Two, we wanted to examine the family dynamics and pathology of these "characters" in a form not usually attempted by the many other more scholarly or journalistic books written about these people, to whom for six years we have had numerous occasions to refer, with varying degrees of disbelief, disgust, and dismay, as "these people."

By this we don't mean "the ruling class" or "WASP aristocrats" or "non-Jews" or even "Republicans." We can live with all of them. Well, most of them. In any case, the rich are always with us, and some of our best friends are Gentiles.

No, by "these people" we mean *these* people — this family, with its scrubbed, boyish men and prim, nice-mommy women and naughty, "high-spirited" kids. Usually, when we tried to express our feelings and thoughts about this all-American aristocratic clan, words failed us. English words, anyway.

And so we reached for Yiddish. A word in English might strike a clear note, but a word in Yiddish sounds a complex chord, three or four or five notes at once, combining emotional accuracy, psychological analysis, sociological observation, and an acknowledgment of the exigencies confronted by every individual who has to live in a world formed, before he got there, by history.

How did Yiddish get that way? Possibly by being a language of outsiders, a semi-official, homemade synthesis of German, Slavic, and Hebrew (and, by now, English). When you're a minority, surrounded by a dominant culture aware of (if not hostile to) your otherness, you become self-conscious — and careful. You speak to each other in code dense with personal meaning. Yiddish arose, then, as the language of a people rather than as the language of a nation or an empire. (And when the Jews became a nation, God forbid they should have established world-famous Yiddish as the national language. No, they had to get even more private and esoteric, and revert to ancient, scary Hebrew.)

The language of outsiders applied to the most

insidery insiders of them all; the language forged in the hottest fires of European Jewish tragedy applied to the gin-and-tonic cool beneficiaries of American Protestant entitlement and privilege; the language whose every subtext is the tension between the personal and the social applied to a family for whom private financial gain and public political success have always seemed as inseparably symbiotic as chicken soup and matzoh balls — yes, Yiddish would be perfect.

As for our story, well, we had in mind a rollicking family drama, where some good old-fashioned sibling rivalry, combined with some good old-fashioned oedipal conflict would equal a tiny insight into the formation of the character of our nation's leader.

In so doing, we had great help from *our* people, and it's a pleasure to acknowledge them.

Thanks to:

Our illustrator, Larry Ruppert, for his patience as well as his enormous talent and simpatico worldview.

Our agent, Paul Bresnick, for a string of base hits and home runs we hope will never stop.

Our Yiddish language adviser, Faith Jones, for knowing when to insist and when to indulge us.

Our main Yiddish source, Michael D. Fein, whose web site (www.pass.to/glossary/) was invaluable, exhaustive, and exhausting.

Our publisher, Michael Pietsch, for behaving so handsomely with regard to that spot of bother in connection with our previous Yiddish book.

And, especially, to our editor, Terry Adams (and his irreplaceable assistant, Sarah Brennan), for a combination of intelligence, taste, diligence, good humor, and all-around wonderfulness. It is they who make it possible for us to say, with complete sincerity, that "after twelve drafts it writes itself."

Finally, profound thanks to our new friend (and "biggest fan") Eleanor Allen, from whose possibly facetious email comment this project developed. It would not exist without her.

— E.W.

I couldn't agree more.

— B. D.

Glossary of Yiddish Words

NOTE: Some spellings are in direct contravention of the (excellent, sensible) advice of our Yiddish adviser, Faith Jones, of the New York Public Library. In those cases we sacrificed technical correctness for phonetic familiarity: we wanted the words to appear as we, and presumably our readers, are used to hearing them. The term Yinglish *refers to the grafting onto Yiddish of English spellings, suffixes, conjugations, etc. The pronunciation instructions embody the opposite of official dictionary conventions, i.e., we made them up.*

af tsores (AHF TSOR-ress) — adv. In trouble, in hot water. "Poor John McCain. When he talks at Liberty University, where the students read the Bible, he's fine. But when he talks at the New

School, where the students read the newspaper, he's *af tsores*."

Alts iz gut (AHLTS eez GOOT, rhyming with "boot") — expression. All is good. All is well. Everything's okay. "They sent out a memo at Fox News. It seems that 'Fair and Balanced' was too liberal, it sent the wrong message to the terrorists, and it didn't support the troops. The new slogan is '*Alts iz gut*.'"

Azoy vert dos kichl tzekrochen (Ah-ZOY VAIRT doss KICH-l tzeh-KROCH-en, with both *ch*'s being guttural) — expression. Lit., "That's the way the cookie crumbles." Coincidence? That a Yiddish expression has an exact English counterpart? No: This is the only term we've heard of that started out in English and, in the U.S., morphed into "a Yiddish expression." (As the Jewish epistemologist said, "Go know!") "The EPA changed its web site. The old one said 'Thirty-five years of protecting Human Health and the Environment.' The new one says '*Azoy vert dos kichl tzekrochen*.'"

Bist meshugeh? (BIST meh-SHOO-geh?) — rhetorical question. Lit., "Are you crazy?" Thus, Are you nuts? Are you kidding or what? "Barbara

Walters did a special with the president and the first lady. When she asked Mr. Bush why he wanted to be president, he said, 'I was put here by God.' Then she asked God if that was true, and He said, '*Bist meshugeh?*'"

brocheh (BRUH-cheh, with the guttural *ch*) — n. A blessing, a benison. "As John Kerry might have said, 'I believe that, ultimately, it was a good thing that the Republicans stole the election from me. Otherwise I would have had to clean up their mess. My beautiful wife, Teresa, and I agree: it was a *brocheh* in disguise.'"

chalushisdick (chah-LUSH-iz-dik, with the *ch* being guttural) — adj. Nauseating, sickening. "Brit Hume spoke at the B'nai Brith. Their Interfaith Dinner, with the prime rib. *Chalushisdick!* Although the prime rib wasn't bad."

chazerai (CHAH-zer-EYE, with the *ch* being guttural) — n. Lit., "piggish," the behavior of a pig. Thus, filth, mess. "Listen, don't kid yourself — if it were up to him, Alberto Gonzales, the so-called Attorney General, would cancel the Bill of Rights and then put it up for sale on eBay with all the other *chazerai*."

chutzpah (CHOOTS [rhymes with "puts"; guttural *ch*]-pah) — n. Unmitigated gall, brazen nerve. "Newt Gingrich tried to finalize the divorce from his first wife while she was in the hospital fighting uterine cancer. That's selfishness. Then he harped on 'family values' while having an affair with a Congressional aide during his second marriage, used tax-exempt charitable donations for partisan political purposes, and gave false statements to the House Ethics Committee. That's hypocrisy. Now he's thinking of running for president. That's *chutzpah*."

epes (EH-piss) — adv. Somewhat, to an extent, a little. "What do the Republicans mean by a 'culture of life'? It means you revere the existence of a clump of a hundred cells in a freezer, but you think it's great to kill thousands of actual people with Shock and Awe when you don't need to. It means, let's face it, that you're *epes* insane."

farbissenah (fahr-BISS-en-nah; fem. Masc. is far-bissiner) — adj., n. Sourpuss, truculent, "crabby" or "a crab." "I don't see how anyone can confuse Mary Magdalene and Mary Matalin. One was a prostitute and Jesus's girlfriend. The other is a Republican and a *farbissenah*."

farfalen (fahr-FAH-len) — adj. Lost, doomed. "Expecting a Republican Congress to pass a decent ethics bill? Forget Mission: Impossible. Try Mission: *Farfalen*."

farkaktah (fahr-KOK-teh) — adj. Lit., "shitty, covered in shit." Lousy, screwed up. "The note of congratulations that Scalia sent to Alito on his confirmation said, 'Welcome to the Supreme Court. With your arrival we conservatives are firmly in control, and I look forward to working with you to finally do something about that *farkaktah* Constitution.'"

farklemt (fahr-KLEMT) — adj. Emotional, choked up. Can also mean depressed. "That Sean Hannity — when he opens those damp puppy-dog eyes and gets all *farklemt* about defending some liar or criminal — it's adorable, at first. And then you have to throw up."

farshlugginer (fahr-SHLUGG-in-er) — adj. Refers to something mixed up or shaken. Thus, something of dubious or little value. "The poor Afghanis. The *farshlugginer* Taliban are back. Thank God *we* don't live in a country heavily influenced by religious fundamentalists."

Farshtayst? (fahr-STAYST) — v. Understand? Got it? "Look, for the last time: the terrorists hate us because of our freedoms. So we're destroying those freedoms, with wiretaps and mass detentions and intimidating the press and smearing whistle blowers and so forth, so they won't hate us as much. Then they'll stop attacking us. Eventually we won't have to be afraid of *any* terrorists *anymore*, and all we'll have to be afraid of is our own government. *Farshtayst?*"

faygelahs (FAY-geh-lehs) — n. Lit., "little birds," colloq. for gay men. Can be pejorative, but not necessarily. A "Yinglish" combination of Yiddish (*faygelah*) and the English *s* to denote the plural.

> LOG CABIN REPUBLICAN #1: I came out to my mother last night. She was devastated. She said, "Don't tell your father, it will kill him. I won't be able to show my face in town, so I hope you're satisfied. In fact, no, I don't believe it. It's just a phase. How could you do this to us? It's just so *wrong*. It's *wrong*."
>
> LOG CABIN REPUBLICAN #2: Wait a minute. I thought your mother once said, "I know you're a *faygelah*, it's fine."
>
> LOG CABIN REPUBLICAN #1: She did. I finally had to tell her I'm a Republican.

finagler (fih-NAY-glur) — n. A schemer, a manipulator. Not really a Yiddish word (it might be Scots!) but everyone thinks it is, and by now it might as well be. "We got tickets to the new musical about Jack Abramoff: *Finagler on the Roof.*"

genug (geh-NOOG, with hard *g*'s and the final syllable rhyming with the "oog" in "boogie-woogie") — adj. Enough. Or, better, "enough, already." Usually used as a beseeching command. "All these ethics investigations and wiretap hearings and grand jury appearances and intelligence committee meetings — *genug*. Just throw the bastards in jail."

geshrai (geh-SHRY) — v., n. Cry, wail, scream. "Russ Feingold is so disgusted with his fellow Democrats, when you call his office and they put you on hold, you hear a recording of him singing 'It's My Party and I'll *Geshrai* If I Want To.'"

goen (goin', as in "Everything's goin' my way.") — n. Genius. "That Dick Cheney — what a *goen*. Severs all his ties with Halliburton and can *still* make a bundle from them."

gornisht helfn (GORE-nisht HELF-'n) — adv. Lit., "no help," useless. "People who say there's no difference between the two political parties are crazy. The Republicans are greedy, corrupt, lying, warmongering, hypocritical bastards. The Democrats are just *gornisht helfn*."

goyim (GOY-y'm) — n. Lit., "nations," used to mean Gentiles, non-Jews. "I'm telling you, this Hamas victory in the Palestinian election...it's not good. Even the *goyim* are worried."

hekdish (HEK-dish; can be pronounced HEG-dish) — n. A mess; a decrepit place, a slum.

> MOLLY: Talk about a complete *hekdish* — the city is built on a swamp, it's unbelievably humid, it's full of black people who are mostly poor, and everywhere you look you see a government that is completely corrupt.
>
> ROSE: I know. And then that terrible hurricane and that business with the levees.
>
> MOLLY: What levees? I'm talking about Washington, DC.

in mitt'n drinen (in MIT'n DRIN'n) — adv. phrase. Suddenly, in the middle of, along with everything else. "There's good news and bad news about evolution. The good news is, the creationists are wrong, intelligent design is baloney, and evolution is real. The bad news is, after 200,000 years of *homo sapiens* evolution and refinement and getting smarter and developing superior skills and evolving a big brain and everything, *in mitt'n drinen* we get Rush Limbaugh. Now we have to start all over."

kaporah (kah-PORE-ah) — n. Disaster, catastrophe. "If Hillary gets the nomination, it will be a victory for her, a triumph for women, and a *kaporah* for the Democrats "

kinder (KIN-der) — n. Pl. of "kind" (rhymes with "skinned"), meaning child. Children, kids. "Reality TV pretends to be real, but it isn't. So we don't watch it in front of the *kinder*. If they really need to see something that's staged, manipulated, and made up, we turn on network news."

kishkes (KISH-kehs) — n. Lit., "innards." Also hose or pipe. Kishke is a kind of sausage stuffed into derma (either beef intestines or turkey neck skin) with flour, onions, and spices. "I don't know about you, but I have had it up to my *kishkes* with

Diane Feinstein, with her conservative voting and her Republican hair."

Kush mir in tuchas (KOOSH [rhymes with "bush"] MEER in TOOCH-us [rhymes with "book us" but with guttural *ch*] — expression. Lit., "Kiss my ass." "They have a very vigorous two-party system in Ohio. Kenneth Blackwell is the Secretary of State, and he's given each party its own special guidelines for elections. For the Democrats, it's '*Kush mir in tuchas*.' For the Republicans, it's 'All you can vote, plus free parking.'"

loch in kop (LUCH [with guttural *ch*] in-kup) — n. Lit., "hole in the head." We found the full text of Scooter Libby's note to Judith Miller: "You went into jail in the summer. It is fall now. You will have stories to cover — Iraqi elections and suicide bombers, biological threats and the Iranian nuclear program. Out west, where you vacation, the aspens will already be turning. They turn in clusters, because their roots connect them. Come back to work — and life. Until then, you will remain in my thoughts and prayers. P.S. Lose my number. I need you now like I need a *loch in kop*."

macher (MAH-cher, with guttural *ch*) — n. Big shot, a mover and a shaker, a player.

> Conservative *macher* Santorum
> Said, "Weddings for gays? I deplore 'em.
> Their marital smooches
> Bring sex with the pooches!"
> Now most Pennsylvanians abhor 'im.

Mazel tov (MAH-z'l tuv) — expression. Lit., "good luck." Used to convey congratulations. Can sometimes imply special merit — not only "Good for you!" but also "because you deserve it."

> MEL: Good news for the election in 2008! I just got off the phone with the Democratic National Committee. We're gonna monitor every polling place in the country. We're gonna make sure every machine produces a paper receipt. We're gonna monitor the exit polls everywhere and if the numbers don't match we're gonna jump all over it! We're gonna make sure there's no purging of the voter rolls. We're gonna have computer experts on call twenty-four/seven! We are gonna be ready!

MOE: *Mazel tov.* Now all you need is a candidate.

megillah (meh-GILL-luh, with a hard *g*) — n. A long story, a tediously lengthy or complicated recounting.

CHILD: Mommy, how did George Bush get to be president?

MOTHER: Oh, it's a whole *megillah* about Ralph Nader, and Florida, and hanging chads, and purging Democratic voters, and the Supreme Court choosing the president instead of letting votes be counted —

CHILD: No, not that time.

MOTHER: Oh, well, that's a whole different *megillah* about lying about 9/11, and lying about Iraq, and the Swift Boat liars lying about John Kerry, and the press just repeating the endless Republican lies, and the rigged Diebold machines —

CHILD: No, not that time.

MOTHER: Oh, well, that's because of the fake Al Qaeda threats, and Ruth Ginsberg dying, and NSA wiretaps and blackmailing Judge Breyer, and the president shutting down Congress and declaring martial law ... Look, sweetie, it's a whole long *megillah* you don't have to worry about. Now just study your Mandarin and get a good night's sleep. Remember we're invading Canada in the morning.

Nifter-schmifter, a leben macht er? (NIF-ter SHMIF-ter ah LAY-ben MACHT er, with a guttural *ch*) — colloq. expression. "What difference does it make (or Who cares), as long as he makes a living?" Pure Yinglish. "They asked Barbara Bush what she had to say about the fact that her son will go down as the most evil, corrupt, dishonest, and destructive president in U.S. history, and she put a nice, positive spin on the whole thing. She said, '*Nifter-schmifter, a leben macht er?*'"

nudnik (NOOD [rhymes with "good"] –nik) — n. A pest, a bore, a nuisance. "Of *course* Colin Powell will write another book, and I have the title all ready. *Nudnik Like Me.*"

ongeshtopt mit gelt (AHNG-gih-shtopt mit GELT, where both *g*'s are hard) — colloq. phrase. Lit., "stuffed with money." Rich, wealthy, "rolling in it." "Listen, if the United States is so *ongeshtopt mit gelt* that we can spend ten billion dollars a month to fight the insurgents in Iraq, why can't we just pay them five billion a month to stop shooting each other already? That's called diplomacy."

Oy (rhymes with "boy") — expression of dismay, surprise, fear, etc. "Oh no." "Oh dear." "Uh-oh..."

> MEL: *Oy*, Jeb Bush may run for president in 2012.
>
> MOE: Well, he can't be any worse than George. Do you really think it would be so terrible?
>
> MEL: What part of "*oy*" don't you understand?

shepn naches (SHEP'n NAH-chus, with a guttural *ch*) — v. phrase. Derive satisfaction, gratification, or pleasure, especially from children or grandchildren. (The word *shept* is the imperative.) "Norman Podhoretz is a neo-con who's part of the Project for the New American Century — the loonies who sent us into Iraq. His son John wrote a book about what a great president Bush is. See? Even a horse's ass can find a way to *shepn naches*."

sheyna maidl (SHAY-nuh MAY-d'l) — n. Lit.,

"pretty girl." (The *s* plural ending in *sheyna maidls* is an English add-on.)

> SCIENTIST #1: If we could create the perfect artificial woman for Republicans, we could make a fortune!
>
> SCIENTIST #2: You're right. OK, what would they think is a real *sheyna maidl?* Let's see: She would have to be a little bit of a dominatrix, and be skinny as a boy, for their latent homosexual fantasies. And she'd say or do anything to make a buck.
>
> SCIENTIST #1: Brilliant. But what shall we call her?
>
> SCIENTIST #2: Got it. *Ann Coulter.*

shikker (SHIK-er) — n. Drunk, drunkard. "What's the difference between a *shikker* and Bill O'Reilly? The *shikker* has a few drinks before he acts nasty, abusive, bullying, and maudlin. Bill O'Reilly has a few drinks afterward."

shiksa (SHIK-sah) — n. A non-Jewish female.

> GOLDIE: So, Rose, they might want this Condoleezza Rice to run for president. But I couldn't

vote for a woman who isn't Jewish. What do you think?

ROSE: She's black, she's a liar, she doesn't have a boyfriend or a husband, so everybody thinks she's a lesbian, and she's in charge of the foreign policy of a completely dishonest and corrupt and incompetent administration — believe me, being a *shiksa* is the least of her problems.

shlimazel (shlih-MAHZ-'zl) — n. A luckless person, a hapless victim, a chump. "Everybody knows you can't have a *shlimazel* without a *shlemiel*. That's why the traditional definition is, the *shlemiel* is the guy who puts on a flight suit and struts around an aircraft carrier and declares 'Mission: Accomplished' when it's hardly even begun... and the *shlimazel* is Donald Rumsfeld."

shluf (shluf, rhymes with "hoof") — n., v. Sleep, nap. To sleep or take a nap. "Reagan, as we know, took too many *shlufs*. Bush, we should be so lucky, should take one big *shluf* and not wake up."

shlumperdik (SHLUM-per-dik) — adj. Lit., "dowdy." Messy, untidy. "How did Karl Rove get out of being indicted by Fitzgerald? By going back to the grand jury over and over, changing his story, remembering what he forgot, forgetting what he didn't remember, finding an e-mail he didn't have, having an e-mail he couldn't find — it was the *Shlumperdik* Defense, and it worked like a charm."

shmegegge (shmeh-GEGG-ee, with hard *g*'s) — n. A buffoon, an idiot, a fool. "That Joe Lieberman — he's such a *shmegegge* even the Democrats won't vote for him."

shmendrik (SHMEN-drik) — n. A nincompoop; an inept person. "I don't want to say that the National Guard is overextended in Iraq, but that *shmendrik* Michael Chertoff just announced that the next time there's a hurricane in New Orleans, they're sending in the Boy Scouts, the Campfire Girls, and the Mickey Mouse Club."

shpotzir (shpot-SEER) — v. Lit., "to hike." To wander, stroll, take a walk. "The White House is complaining that the press isn't telling all the good news about Iraq. And they're right. Before we invaded, the Sunnis were oppressing the Shia and the Kurds. Now you can *shpotzir* around Baghdad and watch all three of them killing each other."

shtik (shtik) — n. Lit., "piece." A routine, a "bit," a characteristic piece of acting. "As soon as he accepted the job of press secretary, Tony Snow said he wasn't going to 'drink the Kool-Aid.' He sure got that *shtik* down fast."

shvants (shvahnts — rhymes with "Hans" with an added *t*) — n. Slang for penis. "What's the difference between Clinton and Bush? Clinton was overly influenced by his *shvants*, and Bush is overly influenced by his Dick."

Shvayg (shvaig; rhymes with the first syllable in "tiger") — v. imperative. "Be quiet," "Shut up," "Pipe down," etc. Stronger than "Ssshh!" but milder than "Shut the f— up!" "What did the U.S. say when the Germans told them that their intelligence about Iraq's nukes was all wrong? '*Shvayg*. It doesn't matter.'"

shver (shvare) — n. Father-in-law. "You want a nightmare? Go marry one of the vice-president's daughters. You get to call Lynn Cheney 'mother' and have Darth Vader for a *shver*."

S' iz geven a fargenign aykh tsu zen (Siz geh-VEN ah FAHR-gen-i-gen EICH tzu zen, with all hard *g*'s) — Lit., "It was a pleasure seeing you."

MOE: I'll take Yiddish phrases for 400, Alex.

ALEX TREBEK: Yiddish for four hundred...
"*S' iz geven a fargenign aykh tsu zen.*"

MOE: Oh, yeah, I know this. Uh — "What did
so-called Dr. Bill Frist not say when he didn't go
to examine Terry Schiavo and diagnosed her as
being not brain-dead, which she was?"

ALEX TREBEK: That is correct.

tchotchkies (CHAHCH-keez) — n. Knickknacks,
doodads, miscellaneous decorative or personal
items. "The Bush administration corrupts everything it touches. The Medal of Freedom used to
mean something. Then they gave it to George
Tenet. Believe me, when I get one it's going right
on the bookshelf in the den with the other
tchotchkies."

therapy schmerapy (therapy SHMARE-a-pee) —
adj. phrase. The addition of *schm* to the front of a
word (regardless of its part of speech; can be
applied to nouns, verbs, adverbs, etc.) minimizes
and dismisses the original word. "Obviously the
Republican Party has lost its mind. But George

Soros has donated enough money to send it to therapy. Look, *therapy schmerapy*. For that kind of money we can start a third party and buy everyone a Prius."

tuchas leker (TOOCH-us [rhymes with "book us," but with guttural *ch*] LEK-er) — n. Lit., "ass licker." Ass-kisser, brown-noser, obsequious fawner. "The administration prizes people who are loyal. Stupid, incompetent, corrupt — doesn't matter. As long as they're loyal. What does 'loyal' mean? It's Texan for '*tuchas leker*.'"

Umbashrien! (OOHM bah SHRINE) — expression. God forbid!

MOE: The Republicans have announced their ticket for the 2008 election. For president, Satan.

MEL: We've had worse.

MOE: For vice-president, Pat Robertson.

MEL: *Umbashrien!*

umglick (OOHM-glik) — n. Lit., "accident." A born loser, an unlucky one. "No matter what you think of him as president, you have to admit he's more than just an *umglick*. He's the Umglick-in-Chief!"

Zeyer sheyn gezogt! (ZIRE SHANE geh-ZOGT, with a hard *g*) — expression. Well said! "I couldn't bring myself to end the seder with 'Next year in Jerusalem.' So instead I made up on the spot, 'Next year at the impeachment!' and everybody raised their glasses and said, *'Zeyer sheyn gezogt!'* And then, of course, *Omeyn*."

Mazel tov, Bar and Poppy!

About the Authors

ELLIS WEINER is author of *The Joy of Worry; Drop Dead, My Lovely; The Big Boat to Bye-Bye;* and *Santa Lives! Five Conclusive Arguments for the Existence of Santa Claus*. He can sometimes be found ranting and raving, in a nice way, on the online blog The Huffington Post.

BARBARA DAVILMAN writes television scripts for sitcoms, reality shows, and TV movies. She has also forged a second career as a prolific writer of letters to the editors of the *Los Angeles Times*, the *New York Times*, and other prestigious journals.

Somehow they managed to put these careers aside and, together, write *Yiddish with Dick and Jane*.

LARRY RUPPERT was born at the tender age of zero in a small Hungarian village. With no serious goals in mind, he attended the Layton School of Art in Milwaukee and became an artist. He has, among other things, illustrated more than two dozen children's books. Of all the truths his parents spoke, "You cannot draw all the time" was not one of them.